TH

BOOKS BY STUART WILDE

Miracles
The Force
Affirmations
The Quickening
The Trick To Money
is Having Some
} The Taos Quintet

Life Was Never Meant To Be A
Struggle
Secrets of Life
Whispering Winds of Change Vol.1

THE SECRETS
OF LIFE

Stuart Wilde

Hay House, Inc.
Carson, CA

Copyright ©1990 by Stuart Wilde

Published and distributed in the United States by:

Hay House, Inc., 1154 E. Dominguez St., P.O. Box 6204, Carson, CA 90749-6204

Book design by John Patrick Lamkin
Illustrations by Stephen Smith

Library of Congress Cataloging-in-Publication Data

Wilde, Stuart, 1946-
    The secrets of life / Stuart Wilde.
       p.   cm.
    Originally published: Taos, N.M., USA : White Dove International, 1991
    ISBN 1-56170-164-5 (tradepaper)
    1. Conduct of life. I. Title.
    [BJ1581.2.W52 1995]
    131–dc20   94-45486
                                                                 CIP

ISBN 1-56170-164-5

99 98 97 96 95 6 5 4 3 2

First Published in 1990 by Nacson & Sons, Pty., Sydney, Australia
Second Printing, January 1995, by Hay House, Inc.

Printed in the United States of America

I dedicate this book
to my dear friend
Leon Nacson.

Dear Friends,

I have put together in this book, *The Secrets of Life*, some thoughts and ideas that form the basic structure of my philosophy on how to develop a more liberated mind-set and thus a more carefree and delightful life. The quotes are from my books and my unpublished writings. In addition, I have included excerpts from TV and radio shows that I have done over the years and from newspaper interviews or from articles I have written.

Open the book anyplace and start reading. Usually you will find that the first few pages you read will contain some helpful hints to some aspect of your life that is currently on your mind. Somehow, the synchronicity of life always leads us to what it is that we need to know. So if you are like me and you want your spiritual concepts on the "hurry up" this book will suit you perfectly.

When you think about it, there are only about a dozen or so concepts in life that you are ever going to need, like stay balanced, develop perception, become detached, concentrate on what's real, act powerfully, believe in yourself and a few others. Once you clutch these to your breast, you set yourself free. And that should be the primary object of your selected path in life, for any philosophy that you can't "get" in two minutes flat and haul down to the bank or up to the airport, ain't worth having, in my view anyway.

See ya on down the line.

Sincerely,

THE SECRETS OF LIFE

THE SECRETS OF LIFE

ON DEDICATION

T IS rare that you meet a person who is truly dedicated. When you do, you will find that he or she is almost always very successful. Dedication is the warrior's prayer unto himself. It is a mode of fierce concentration, in which you become so attached and devoted to your cause that eventually life has to give you everything that you desire. Dedication is vital. You have to live your life like a warrior and live and breathe your ambitions.

THE SECRETS OF LIFE

ON PERSERVERANCE

YOU HAVE to be ready to take advantage of situations as and when they arise. Perseverance allows you to hold on while the Universal Law delivers.

ON CHALLENGING YOURSELF

You see, just getting through life is not enough. If you have any kind of real goal you will want to challenge yourself. People find a little rut to follow and they stick to it. This is because the mind does not like spontaneity or change. People tend to create patterns they are comfortable with and they pursue that path day-in and day-out. Everything is fine for twenty-seven years, and then one day there is a bear on the path and it eats them.

ON THE SACREDNESS OF THINGS

THE THINGS you believe in are the baggage you carry with you in your life. The true sage believes in nothing, other than the sacredness of all things. He lives in the spontaneity of energy. He defends nothing nor judges anything. His world is eternal and infinite. He sees beauty in all things and he accepts the ways of man, including restriction and strife. He knows that without constraints there would be no challenge.

ON OPPORTUNITY

F YOU move toward your goals, expressing all your power, opportunity will find you as a result of your actions. For by riding your energy, knowing and believing your Higher Self is with you, you will be in the right place at the right time. But make the first move, taking constant care to purify and review your life; move from negative habits into the fortress of light. Discipline is the horse you ride.

ON SEEING THINGS
AS PERFECT

WE CANNOT go beyond the earth plane while criticizing it, for it serves us, as all restriction does. To go beyond the earth plane you have to be able to accept it, to see beauty within it no matter what, to see it as perfect. Then you develop the spiritual maturity to leave things as they are, under-standing that the Force knows what it is doing.

THE SECRETS OF LIFE

ON "WHERE THE HELL AM I?"

IF YOU think about it, none of us are actually here on the earth. For we are not our bodies or our minds—rather, we are a Higher Self in a body. It is as if we are in a space suit peering out at a strange world. But the "real you" has never landed. Yet in bouncing about on this "moon-like" surface you tend to forget that the space suit is not the real you. Meanwhile the Mother Ship is up there all the time beaming us guidance on how to keep the space suit in one piece and how to get the most out of our "earthwalk". The overall control mechanism is beyond earth. Life is just an experiment to see how well you can cope. It's all a matter of gathering experiences for other adventures.

ON DIMENSIONS

THE HIGHER SELF is subtle. It does not bang you on the head with a plank. It allows gradual growth as you discover a deeper and deeper meaning to the world around you. Dimensions are inward; they unfold to energy like those Chinese dolls that you take apart to find another doll inside, and yet another and so on. The only thing that bars you from experiencing those infinite inner spaces is incompatibility between your energy and the dimension you wish to experience.

ON THE HIGHER SELF

THE HIGHER SELF is a collective body of energy. Within it is all the knowledge that you will ever need, and through it you can experience a limitless understanding of the physical plane as well as the "unseen dimensions" that lie close at hand. At the beginning of time the Higher Self individualized from the God Force or Living Spirit and it began to grow and divide itself into more and more experiences. Some of the things it has been are your past lives, but even before it entered the human form it had experiences that would help it adjust to the vibrational force of the physical plane. So it experienced energy as lesser forms: as electricity, as light and color, as sound. It is interesting to think that there is evolution in the sound of a pebble going over a cliff or that within a flower there are countless dimensions of evolution—Higher Selves experiencing training, destined perhaps one day to be human.

ON THE GOD FORCE

HE GOD FORCE is always moving toward you. It is like a warm, divine wind that is blowing in your direction. If you want to call it an Egyptian prince, fine, but in a way understand it's just a power. It's more than intuition. It's an inner knowing that grows because you understand its infinity and you know that the Force is within you. It will teach you hour by hour, day by day. It'll show you the people you need to be associated with. It'll show you the suitcases you need to unlatch and throw off the cart. It shows you freshness. It shows you the way. The reason it teaches you is because at this point you are basically beyond the earth experience. So

THE SECRETS OF LIFE

you've got to have something to help you otherwise you would flounder. But you will never touch it, taste it, smell it or see it, but it is with you at this very minute. As you begin to trust this power it will lead you step by step—it knows. How does it know? It knows because it is all-knowing and powerful so it seeks the same for every part of itself and you are one of those parts. It will take you to the next person. It will take you to the next place. It knows what parts of yourself that you need to work on in order to become stronger. If you work on them and change those aspects then suddenly a door opens. There's a whole new dimension waitin' for you but it doesn't want you comin' in with any old stuff. Once you get rid of the stuff, in you come.

THE SECRETS OF LIFE

ON DISCIPLINE AT DAWN

BY REFRESHING yourself through silence and nature, you constantly revitalize the inner you. Dawn is your strongest hour. If you can rise in time to meet the day, that effort becomes a discipline that you use for establishing control. Use the time to project yourself mentally into the day. As you center your mind, the power of your Higher Self goes out and surrounds the events you will meet, acting as a spiritual forerunner, enlivening energy in front of you. By setting up your day before the rest of the world has risen, you establish an energy that cannot be overwhelmed by the negativity of others.

THE SECRETS OF LIFE

ON ESTABLISHING CONTROL

THE KEY to establishing control is to spend a part of each day completely alone. Use the time to review your feelings and concerns—allow an emotional maturity to develop whereby you deeply understand that nothing is real. The old Taoist sages, who understood the importance of maintaining control at all times and avoiding confrontation, taught their students that their life is like a stick floating down a river and that interpersonal strife snags it, bringing your progress to a standstill. Confrontation fuels the ego and strengthens the power of the subconscious over your affairs. The sage walks away, the fool stands and fights.

THE SECRETS OF LIFE

ON TRANSCENDING

THERE IS no shortcut to completing your earth experience. You will have to experience all of it, for metaphysically, you can only go beyond something by going through it. Your life builds upon a pattern and eventually that pattern sets you free.

THE SECRETS OF LIFE

ON UNDERSTANDING YOUR LIFE

HIS LIFETIME is yours. You may be involved in relationships and love others, but basically what you make of your life and how you pass through it is your evolution. That is why adversity is so useful. In desperation, we begin to pull on our unlimited power and we realize that anything can be changed, that suffering is a product of the inner self, and, by looking at our inner selves, we can transform ourselves. To overcome something once and for all means going within yourself to discover the real causes of the disturbance. This process or discovery will allow you more energy, which you can use to create the things you want in your life.

THE SECRETS OF LIFE

ON THE NATURE OF BELIEFS

 N DAILY life, your feelings, thoughts, and attitudes are your order form, so before you decide to change your present conditions you will have to be very sure of what you want from life. The currency with which you are going to pay for it is belief. To create something with absolute certainty you have to establish the feeling within you that it has already been granted— that the condition you desire is already a part of your life.

THE SECRETS OF LIFE

ON ASSESSING
YOUR PLANS

SK YOURSELF prior to committing to anything, "Do I have the wherewithal to pull it off and do I know what I am getting into?" What is your motivation for taking action? What is the level of your commitment and do you actually want the end result or are you going for something else instead? Are you trying to capture a castle you don't really need or want?

THE SECRETS OF LIFE

ON CONCENTRATION

CONCENTRATION IS a key discipline in personal growth and development. Most everything else is meaningless. Your power rests where your consciousness flows. When you are centered and concentrating on what you are doing, not only do you derive more from your actions but also all of your power, both inner and outer, is being used to empower your actions. If you train the laser light of your intention in a direction, you empower that direction with your energy. Through concentration you become powerful. Force your mind to concentrate and you have won a battle over struggle.

THE SECRETS OF LIFE

ON OVER-THINKING

IF YOU'RE wondering—don't wonder. Over-thinking on life is a trap. Get out of it. There usually isn't an explanation to much of what happens.

ON RELATIONSHIPS

ET OUT of any situation that endorses negativity, that causes you imbalance. People come together in relationships for growth, not life. If a relationship sustains you, if you are both growing from it, if it's beautiful and it has energy, you're together for good. If not, either fix it or ditch it. You don't need situations that don't support you or that lower your energy. You don't owe anything to anyone. The only real responsibility you have is to work on yourself to raise your energy. That will become your gift to the world. Pull back from negative situations and negative people. You don't need to judge them, or try to change them. Just allow them to follow their path.

THE SECRETS OF LIFE

You may want to give them a little shove. But if they won't move, you move. Never mind security.

ON STAYING AWAKE

OFTEN WE are so busy "doing" life, we forget to experience it. We end up missing most of it.

Demand of your mind to notice everything all the time. Wake up to your perceptions.

ON THE NATURE
OF THE QUEST

I F SOMEBODY suggests something to you that seems terribly easy, quite often the subconscious mind will like the idea because you're good at it. But, if it's something that seems easy, that you can do well, it's probably not what you need. On the other hand, the uncertainties that you would face by doing something hard will test you in your weakest areas and you will be challenged. A path that will test you can still have a lot of light.

ON GOING BEYOND THE CURRENT SITUATION

A S YOU do your job immaculately, your energy will stand out like a neon light, because almost everyone else is doing a lousy job. Wherever you find yourself right now, do the job immaculately. By doing so you will eventually go beyond it. Bit by bit you energize yourself into various different positions until you reach the point where you really want to be. The light that is guiding you will always show you the next step. That light is always there, at every stage of the path.

THE SECRETS OF LIFE

ON BECOMING CRAFTY

BECOME A crafty Mongol. Never say "Yes" and never say "No." Play the waiting game—control the time frame. When others try to put you on the "hurry up," play dumb. Stall for time. When they try to confront you engage them by drawing them out of their castle. Get them to show you how brilliant they are. Stimulate their ego. Doing so, they will lean toward you. In leaning, they lose balance. Then tap them psychologically or emotionally and before they realize what's happened, they are in open ground with their knickers 'round their ankles, looking silly.

THE SECRETS OF LIFE

ON WALKING SLOWLY

THE TRICK in life is to walk—don't run. Go into every situation with calm, appraising it in the light of your expertise. Doing this you allow yourself freedom. You pull from a reservoir of strength that is very different to the way most people live life. It sets you apart and grants you mystery. People wonder how your life seems so effortless compared to theirs. By having mystery and developing your ways in secret, people grant you a reputation that is actually greater than that which you have achieved so far. That helps you.

THE SECRETS OF LIFE

ON CLARITY

DECIDE WHAT is important to you. Your home, your family, your job— whatever. Then gradually eliminate those things that are superfluous. In doing so, you become even more clear as to what you actually want. That is important, for if you do not know what you want, life reflects back to you uncertainty. If you're one of those people who genuinely doesn't know what they want, begin by eliminating those things that you know you don't want! In simplifying your life, things become clear. From within you come ideas. But first you have to bag the clutter.

THE SECRETS OF LIFE

ON HEALING THE PLANET

HE HEALING of the planet will take place once individuals feel comfortable accepting their reality, wherever it might take them, with the understanding that life is, in effect, a heroic journey of self-realization, not just a quest for self-aggrandizement. Once this thought-form correction takes place, the world will automatically heal itself, and humans will truly experience a Golden Age of creativity, love, and personal fulfillment.

ON COMPETITION

THE SPIRITUAL warrior is not involved in competition. He or she is involved in energy. Once you get into developing energy there is basically no more competition. You are out on your own in the marketplace and you can more or less do what you like and charge what you like.

ON ACCEPTANCE

TO COME to a full and permanent acceptance of evolution here allows the warrior to enter into a purity of spirit that is not normally attained by others. It is that final resignation whereby you settle into an acceptance of what you are, and you rest in the reality of what you are, rather than the fantasy of what you are not. Your acceptance of life is an outpouring of your inner sense of comfort, rather than a by-product of your fortunate circumstances. Purity in the spiritual warrior's sense is a consolidation of power. There is honor and purity in the warrior's quest. In attaining the realization of immortality, the individual accepts his or her destiny as found. The secret is

THE SECRETS OF LIFE

to concentrate on changing yourself gradually, as fast as your inner self can accept that change.

ON METAPHYSICAL STRENGTH

THE MORE powerful you are, the more ability you have to materialize your wants. One's metaphysical strength is like a bank balance. It represents the time lag between what you conceive for your life in your mind and when it actually appears. Wimpy people imagine forever and nothing ever shows up. For the less wimpy variety their thoughts show up in various forms but less than they had hoped for. In the strong ones, events show up more or less immediately. The sage can materialize the burning bush in the flick of a thought form; most others would have difficulty materializing a box of matches over six months.

THE SECRETS OF LIFE

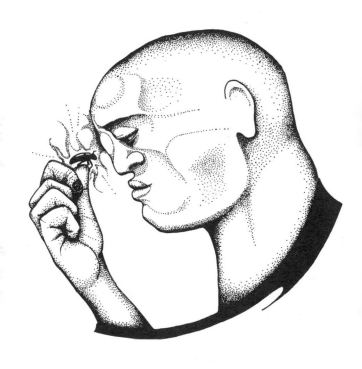

THE SECRETS OF LIFE

ON THE REAL YOU

THE REAL you, the inner you, is pure, very pure. It's loving and it's magnanimous. It understands. It has patience. It is tolerant—it will wait forever while your ego trots all over everywhere trying to figure life out. It's pleasing to remember that back home there is a friend who's waiting for you to stop being silly, who's waiting to welcome you with open arms if and when you show up.

THE SECRETS OF LIFE

ON OPERATING IMMACULATELY

I REMEMBER getting into a taxi in Chicago. If you have ever been to the States, you will know about those Yellow cabs, they are totally revolting. When you crawl in, you think you're going to get some exotic disease just sitting there. The seats are incredibly shiny, so every time the taxi takes a corner, you slide up the other end like a plastic duck in the bath. First you're up by the taps— next, you're up at the round end, and you're having a terrible time swishing about in a tin box! I can't stand taxis, I try to use limos in America—never mind the price, 'cos I prefer something that works and leaves me intact at the end of the journey.

THE SECRETS OF LIFE

Anyway, one day in Chicago it was raining, so I had to hail a taxi in spite of all my reservations. I opened this guy's taxi and to my surprise it was immaculate, utterly immaculate. The driver was this big strong guy and he smiled and said "Hi, man, how're you doing?" I replied, "I'm fine thank you." I got inside his taxi, it was carpeted. That's unheard of in America. Carpeted! There were little candies in a tray and all of the daily newspapers were in a rack. The guy had a stereo system piped through to the back and he was playing soul music, but he said, "Listen, I'm playing soul music, but what kinda music d'you want? You want classical, you want jazz, what do you want? I've got all these tapes." I said,

THE SECRETS OF LIFE

"Try me classical," and he plugs the music in for me. There were little air fresheners. The cab was immaculate. You could eat your breakfast on the floor. The ride was two bucks forty. How much tip are you going to give that guy? You've got to give him five bucks and say, "Keep the change," haven't you? Because, getting in his taxi was a whole energy experience. He told me about Chicago, and life in Chicago, he was an incredibly neat guy. I learned about the black community and how they liked the new mayor, because he was black, and everybody was having a nice time and it was all song and dance in Chicago. I came out feeling exhilarated. What does it cost? You don't give a damn! Now that guy

THE SECRETS OF LIFE

knew metaphysics. He didn't struggle, he understood energy and knew how to turn it into a buck or two.

ON EXPANDING YOURSELF

MOST PEOPLE think raising your energy means meditating and eating stewed veggies. All that stuff helps but there're other ways you can raise your energy fast. Go out and buy experiences for yourself. Do new things that challenge you. Force yourself to go meet new people. Meeting people is vital. Sooner or later you will need a hand up from where you find yourself and someone has to give you that hand. The more someones you know, the more chance you have of making it to the promised land.

THE SECRETS OF LIFE

ON ABUNDANCE

I WANT you to expect that things are going to sustain you. Why shouldn't they? Life sustains itself. Get used to beginning to work with your feelings so that you come out of a powerful energy, a feeling of abundance. That feeling of abundance has nothing to do with how much money you've got. Abundance is saying, "I feel rich in my feelings, I feel rich in the friendships I have, in the love I have, in my intellect; I feel abundant in nature, in the naturalness of all things; I feel strong, and the fact that I haven't got a pot to piss in is a mere aberration." Once you feel abundant you are bound to become it, and that's the secret!

THE SECRETS OF LIFE

ON QUEST AND MONEY

I BELIEVE that we are all on a metaphysical quest. You may not necessarily describe your life in those terms, but I believe we are here to understand ourselves and that includes the physical plane. That means the physical body, mentality, emotions, sexuality, motherhood, fatherhood and cash. You simply have got to have cash—otherwise, the tail wags the dog. The trick to money is having some. There isn't really anything else to it. It amazes me how many people miss that point.

THE SECRETS OF LIFE

ON NOT
QUANTIFYING THINGS

ONCE YOU accept life you can see that everything serves you in some way or other. A lousy meal helps you appreciate and remember a good meal. A defeat strengthens you for the next victory. If you try not to quantify and judge things and accept them as a part of your overall experience you become spiritually mature. All of a sudden that power that should have been yours from the beginning is returned to you. It returns to you in an individuality—a creative stillness that allows you to be, that unshackles you from the restraints that you've created and allows you to explore inside your own individuality.

THE SECRETS OF LIFE

ON RESTRICTION

IF YOUR feelings are closed down and narrow, you eventually pull restriction into your life because what you're putting out is restriction. You might not be aware of it, but restriction is endemic to all our societies. It's taught in school. Everywhere you go—Australia, the West Coast of the United States, Canada, England and back again— you see nothing but control and restriction of the people. It is awesome. But people are used to it. They like it. It's as if somebody came along and they thumped you on the foot every hour with a mallet. The first time you'd be annoyed, really annoyed. But by the second hour you'd be a little less angry. Once they

THE SECRETS OF LIFE

had been thumping you on the foot
every hour on the hour for ten years,
you'd be sitting there thinking, "Oh,
he'll be along in a minute," because
you'd get used to it. You'd think, "Oh,
he's late, what happened to him?"
That's how we are. You can't, unless
you get out and stand back and look
at it, even conceptualize the level of
restriction that you accept into your
life. By opening your heart you are
affirming that you are prepared to
break out.

ON DEVELOPING AN
ALTERNATIVE PHILOSOPHY

IF YOU want an evolution that is different from the tick-tock rhythm of the masses— where you get into an independent control of your financial, spiritual, intellectual destiny, where you can actually motivate yourself in the right direction, you are going to have to develop—whether you like it or not—a philosophy that is diametrically opposed to what the other folk believe. If you are in the consciousness of the masses, you are bound to wind up in the destiny of the masses. You won't want that—take my word for it.

THE SECRETS OF LIFE

ON PRACTICALITY AND FLOW

THERE IS a very subtle balance between being in the flow and trusting that the God Force will bring to you all the things you need, and doing things that will ensure you get what you want. Once you understand that you can say, "I'm in the flow, I trust in the beauty of my own inner light, but I am also doing these thirty-five very practical things to make sure I don't get my rear end mangled."

ON STEPPING BEYOND

FOUR TIMES in a person's life, he or she is offered the chance to step spiritually beyond the confines of the physical plane. Very few accept the offer, for it means you have to control the mind and the negativity of your life, and to discipline yourself into another more spacious reality. At first the transition is like crossing a fast-moving stream—it's tricky, but not hard. If you refuse to take the step the next time you have a chance, it will feel like crossing a raging river. If again you refuse, the power of your mind grows and grows, and making that transition will feel like swimming a very large lake with all the effort and consistency that entails. Finally, the

THE SECRETS OF LIFE

battle for supremacy of your life will take immense strength and it will feel like you have to swim across a great sea. The name of the game is to take your chances early, when they are offered.

ON NOT LETTING PEOPLE TOW YOU BY THE NOSE

A S YOU get more and more independent and more powerful and less in ticktock and more into your own philosophy and alternative ideas, you are not going to give a damn what people think about you. You didn't come down to the earth plane to keep the other 5 billion people happy. Try this: for the next 30 days, don't do anything for anyone without charging for it. When you are asked to give someone a lift to the station, tell them it will cost $10.00. If they ask why, tell them "This week I feel good about myself. This week I'm learning to empower myself, $10.00." And, if they argue, make it $20.00. When you feel OK about charging people, then you can do

THE SECRETS OF LIFE

things for nothing and play the nice guy. For you know that you can include yourself if and when you have to. That's important. Otherwise the world tows you around by the nose.

ON SELF-LOVE

WE'RE CONSTANTLY out there trying to get people to love us. What we're really saying when we're trying to get people to love us is, "I really don't like myself that much at all." Because, if you love yourself— not in an egotistical sense, but you're just satisfied with where you are, you're happy about the fact that you don't have it all together; you're happy about the fact that sometimes you don't show up on time; you're happy about the fact that sometimes you forget to pay your bills; you're happy about the fact that sometimes you get blind drunk, or whatever it is that you do. Then, you can totally

THE SECRETS OF LIFE

accept yourself. Once you accept yourself, everybody else accepts you. It's only when you feel insecure about who you are that other people don't like you. Why? Because your insecurity rattles their insecurity fears. When you're strong they feel safe.

ON ENERGY

A S YOU feel good about yourself, you won't feel bad about charging. The energy inside tick-tock is incredibly sluggish, even if you're in one of the western nations like England, America, or Canada. As you start to raise your energy, you work upon yourself, you work upon discipline and people will be drawn to you. People will show up—I promise you. They will crawl over the walls, under the doors, lower themselves down through the ceiling to be there with you. When they show up, what you have to do is "bill 'em!" You have to be ready to bill 'em. If you can't bill 'em, you'll never make it.

THE SECRETS OF LIFE

ON AVOIDING INDECISION

SEVENTY PERCENT of all the people I've surveyed in seminars don't know what they want. If you do not know what you want, you are putting out into the Universal Law "I don't know what I want," and it reflects back, "Listen mate, if you haven't got a bloody clue, we haven't got a clue either." So, look at that, and get focused. Decide what you want. And life will begin to deliver it to you.

THE SECRETS OF LIFE

ON THE BENEFITS
OF RESTRICTION

RESTRICTION IS good. It serves you. For it binds you into circumstances so that you are forced to work upon yourself. It's sort of an insurance policy that makes sure you don't get out too far ahead of yourself until you are absolutely ready. But once you grow metaphysically the restrictions around you no longer serve you. That's when you need to bag 'em.

THE SECRETS OF LIFE

ON FEAR

ONCE YOU agree to take full responsibility for your life, you may feel scared—and quite rightly so. Once you conceptualize it you'll feel terrified. But it's only the mind that's frightened—the inner you is not. And once you admit that you're scared— it's neat, because first, you understand the frailty of the human condition, and second, you realize that the inner you will have to carry you from this point on. The point where you "click" from living in your mind to trusting the inner you is a major turning point for many.

ON PHILOSOPHIES

WHO SAID that understanding life is hard? Who said it is difficult? The greatest concepts of all time are the simplest. If somebody brings you a philosophy on a cart with books piled high and says "Here, join this," run. If they bring you a philosophy that's written on a few little itty-bitty pieces of paper that say "The pub opens at 6 p.m.," ask, "How do I join?" Because philosophy, the understanding of life, is only energy. It's not the words people say. If they bring you this great big holy book with a big clasp on it and say "Here, kiss this," you reply, "You kiss it, Bozo. I need a good laugh." Philosophy, the inner you, is simple. It is so simple we miss it.

ON SPIRITUAL ENLIGHTENMENT

I DON'T know about you, but I like my spiritual enlightenment on the hurry-up. I don't have time to read 60 volumes of this or that. If you can't explain it to me in 30 seconds it can't be the God Force, in my view anyway.

THE SECRETS OF LIFE

ON THE MORE YOU KNOW
THE LESS YOU KNOW

WE THINK spiritual understanding has got to be a big complication. But in reality, you don't even have to be clever to be spiritual. In fact, the less bright you are, the less trouble you'll have. Because the cleverer you are, the more of an intellectual base you come out of, the more you have to move in and out of the labyrinth of your mind to get to the light. But if you can just intuit it, there it is. Easy.

THE SECRETS OF LIFE.

THE SECRETS OF LIFE

ON LIVING THE LUCID DREAM

WHEN YOU'RE driving to work and there's a guy in front of you doing 15 mph, and you're honkin' and gettin' angry and you're saying, "This idiot, why is he doing 15 mph?"—you should relax and realize that he's doing 15 mph because that's how far he wants to push the pedal. He's got all day to make it down to Safeway and back. He doesn't understand that you're 30 minutes late for work. The fact is, we all have to live in each other's dream. But if somebody is imposing a dream on you that you don't like, move. You don't have to accept their reality. The whole name of the game is to constantly move in and out of positions that you don't

THE SECRETS OF LIFE

like—that are not compatible with your energy—until you find circumstances that you do like. Our feet are the most wonderful gift God ever gave us. They allow us to make selections.

ON PERSONAL WEAKNESSES

DON'T WORRY, you will grow spiritually in spite of any weaknesses you may have. That's the way human evolution is organized. And a good thing, too, for most of us.

THE SECRETS OF LIFE

ON GUILT

ONCE MAN moved from a spiritual relationship with God to an emotional, survival-based relationship with God, then we developed sin. Once we had sin there's only one way we could go: backwards. Because even if you're doing everything OK 99 times out of 100, on the 100th occasion when you forget to fling the virgins off the cliff, you're in trouble. You feel worthless. "Oh my god, the tribe didn't go through the ritual this week." What do you feel when you feel guilty—you feel worthless. Once you have guilt you have weakness.

ON GOING BEYOND THE EARTH PLANE

WHEN YOU move in your mind beyond the day-to-day consciousness of the earth plane, you never tell 'em you've gone. It's easier and safer that way.

THE SECRETS OF LIFE

ON WALKING AWAY

THERE'S A point in your spiritual evolution where you may have to walk away from the old system, otherwise you're constantly being jangled by the dichotomy of who you really are as an infinite being, and what you have to pretend to be in order to fit. The more infinite you become in your spirituality the more difficulty you'll have adapting to a very restrictive, manipulative society.

ON SOCIETIES

RULES SUCK.
In my philosophy
anyway.
I like to be Pope in
my own church.

ON JOY

IN THEORY, joy should be a natural part of our lives. Somehow, isn't it true, we get so caught up in the crazy, frenetic pace of modern living that we get disconnected from that inner part of oneself that naturally rests in a state of equilibrium, in peace, at one with all things? And so, we almost have to make joy a habit, a long-lost friend to see. In the craziness of life, we shouldn't lose sight of the beauty, the calm, and the purpose to things.

ON IT AIN'T THAT SERIOUS

YOU KNOW when you watch people rushin' around—it seems like they're taking life incredibly seriously. They're all hurtlin' about makin' everything mega-important. And yet when you think about it, their seriousness is really a sign of immaturity; it's a sign that says, "I don't feel safe and I don't feel I control my life, so I'm gonna create an incredible bally-hoo around me and everybody else just to make sure we all make it." And yet, seriousness is so childish because life really isn't that serious. When we can back off we see that one result or another doesn't really make that much difference in the long run. And yet, seriousness always comes out of a

THE SECRETS OF LIFE

sense of immaturity, a sense of weakness. And so if you're surrounded by a bunch of people who are incredibly serious what I suggest you do is this: Get a lemon meringue pie and walk into your boss's office and smash it in his face. And say to him, "OI, you silly old twit, back off, what about a little fun in life?"

ON PERSONAL FREEDOM

HE WHOLE function of the evolution of humans on the physical plane as I see it (in what are basically extremely restricted circumstances), is to eventually become free. If you don't win your freedom, you spend the whole of your life in prison. There are prisons of our physical bodies that won't clunk along. There is emotional restriction where you find yourself trapped by circumstances, or the confinement created by the society or family you are from. Or you have to endure restriction because you have no cash and everybody's telling you where to go and what to do. The way to tackle the problem is to select one or two areas that you know you can fix without much effort. Untangling those knots gives you the spaces to build your power so that you can tackle the harder stuff. Eventually you break out of all of the things that bind you.

ON LAW AND FREEDOM

IS A MINUTE of democracy every four years personal freedom? I think not. When you look at the statute books—there're over a million laws there. If you begin to read them today you'd be six foot under before you ever got to the end. Our lives are so restricted there's a law for everything. There's a crossing the street law, a turnin' out the light law and a law for every single move you ever make. And so what do you do about it? I believe the secret is to detach. If you can pull back emotionally from the circumstances of your life you can look at things objectively and see that there's a path through for you. It's my way of making life a little less serious. So, if

THE SECRETS OF LIFE

somebody says to you, "What do you think of the government?" your reply should be, "I try not to." That way, you can get on with your life without being emotionally sucked in to everything that's going on. Personal freedom is a state of mind.

ON BEING IN FLOW

I BELIEVE that life was never really meant to be a struggle—yet somehow we are taught that life is one of effort, hard work, anguish and difficulty, and battling on regardless. And yet, when we look at nature and we look at what is around us, we can see a simplicity and a flow. Does the tiger get up in the morning and say "I'm gonna' try hard today; I'm gonna jog 'round the block and stick alfalfa sprouts up my nose and lob my vitamins and I'm gonna really struggle like crazy and hopefully by lunchtime I'll get something to eat?" No, it doesn't. It just gets up, has a little sniff under its tiger armpits and wanders out into the forest and there at lunchtime on the path is lunch.

THE SECRETS OF LIFE

And, it's the same for you. If you get into flow and you pull away from the emotion of struggling, sure, you may have to drive across town to pick up a check and take it to your bank, but it doesn't have to be anguish—it doesn't have to be laced with emotion. Effort is part of the physical condition. Struggle is effort laced with emotion. And you don't need that.

ON PARTYING

IF YOU'RE not in bed by midnight—come home.

ON WEAK MARRIAGES

THE TRICK to marriage is pickin' a good'un. Because if you're gonna' commit yourself to somebody for the rest of your life, why would you want to hitch up to somebody who's mega-wimpy? You wouldn't. Unless control is your game. Personally, if I were into control, which I am not, I would want to control something that was fun, like the Washington Redskins. What's the thrill in controlling some wimp and four bricks in the suburbs? Stay single, until a good'un comes along. That's the best way.

ON SOUL MATES

THE SECRET for a male is to temper his outgoing sexuality, and to cultivate inner softness, understanding that there is strength in softness. For a female, the key is to accept her position as the custodian of the spiritual, inner energy of the world, for she has a natural spirituality within her. Then, if a spiritual male and a spiritual female come together in a dedication of energy, they can create a powerhouse of light. The challenge is to pull to yourself the spiritual person you need to create the missing link. Here, the key is to work on your body, your nutrition, the quality of your thoughts and actions; to create and maintain a high energy about yourself, then

THE SECRETS OF LIFE

others with a high energy will be
attracted to what you are. You don't
need a slug for a soul mate. Many of
you have tried that; it didn't work.

ON LOVE AND MARRIAGE

JUST BECAUSE you fall in love with somebody is absolutely no reason to marry them. If you put out "send me anyone," you'll usually wind up with a relationship that you don't want.

THE SECRETS OF LIFE

ON POVERTY

POVERTY IS neat because it helps you to understand wealth. After you've done poverty for a couple of twenty years, you wake up one morning and think, "Christ, I've had enough of this." It motivates you to trot off and make a packet.

ON DISEASE

ISEASE IS beautiful. It serves a good purpose. Because if you run your body like a train through the night, where the driver's in the restroom and the whole bloody thing is hurtling down the hill at ninety— what happens is, finally, the body jumps the track. At that point you realize you've got to get the driver out of the restroom and back up to the front of the train. Disease is handy—it stops you from killing yourself.

ON TEACHERS

PEOPLE SAY that as a teacher you should be perfect and set a good example. But that's nuts. If you are perfect you don't need to learn anything and if you don't need to learn anything, you wouldn't need to be a teacher.

ON MAINTAINING YOUR PHILOSOPHY

IF PEOPLE say, "I think your philosophy is the pits," you say, "Well, thank you—I appreciate you sharing your opinion." Then if they say, "I think that what you believe is stupid and you're dumb and you're not righteous and you're not gonna get to heaven and you're gonna have a lousy time," you say, "Thank you for your opinion—it helps me concentrate. I particularly liked the way that cockroach walked around your coffee cup while you were talking about my life. And what threw me into a state of absolute ecstasy was when the cockroach stopped, looked up at me, winked, and then urinated in your coffee. I loved it. I totally loved it."

THE SECRETS OF LIFE

ON HONOR

HE WAY people look at honor makes me laugh. They use it to get sane. The theory is that right-minded people go off to some muddy trench in France and get their bloody liver blown off. And when the guy's sitting there with his liver 45 yards away people say "Well, how do ya feel? " "Honorable, man. I feel real honorable—I'm doin' it for king and country." Now, I am not saying all of those guys are wrong, for they feel a need, but it seems to me there must be an easier way of doing honor.

THE SECRETS OF LIFE

ON LIMITLESSNESS

NCE YOU realize that you are not your body, that you're not your mind, that you're not your emotions, or the nation you were born into, or the color of your skin, or the religion that you believe in, but that you're truly this divine spark within yourself—you become limitless. And, that is the key to mysticism—that is the key to understanding life.

ON DECLARING YOURSELF IN

EVERYTHING IS out there waiting for you. All you have to do is walk up and declare yourself in. No need for permission. You just need the courage to say "Include me in." If you say it with conviction no one challenges you and no one realizes that this is your first day on the job and that you haven't got a clue which way's up.

If you act as if you've been in the game a thousand years no one will guess different.

THE SECRETS OF LIFE

ON TRUTH

RUTH IS my friend.

THE SECRETS OF LIFE

ON THE WAY THINGS ARE

THE WAY things are is the way things are. Accept that. In doing so it sets you free. Then if you don't like the way things are you can set about changing them. But the first point of your empowerment over circumstances is to stop struggling against them and accept them.

THE SECRETS OF LIFE

ON UNDERSTANDING

HERE ARE many things I do not understand. I like it that way. It took me a long time to realize that having to know the answer to everything is a trap. There are loads of things to which there are no real answers. So if your mate Harry ploughs through the front of the Seven-Eleven, you can sit and wonder all day why that happened or you can just accept that it did. Sure there's a reason, but what good will it do to trouble yourself over it? Maybe Harry needed out of the earth plane in a hurry and they are not called "convenience stores" for nothing!

THE SECRETS OF LIFE

ON EVOLUTIONARY EXPERIENCES

WHEN YOU read about some horrific disaster, or whatever it is the press and media are trying to feed you this week, you are concerning yourself with something that is not your reality. It's nothing to do with your evolution. You need to detach from what is going on and look at it from an infinite viewpoint rather than the more finite survival issues that dominate most people's lives. On one level three hundred folk hit a mountain but on another level everyone's infinite so none of them is dead. They all exist in some other dimension. Then you can avoid the emotion and say, "Interesting evolutionary experience."

THE SECRETS OF LIFE

ON STRUGGLE

O JUSTIFY the fact that their lives are out of control, Strugglers like to feel that struggle is noble—that somehow God is pleased with them for struggling. If you were God, you would fall over laughing at that one. The God Force does not ask us to struggle, nor does it ask us to sacrifice ourselves, or to be poor. All of these are conditions man has imposed upon himself, for it is easier to do nothing and struggle than it is to bring forth the creativity from within us and charge for it.

THE SECRETS OF LIFE

ON LIFE

SK YOURSELF, "Am I having a good time, right now?" Having a good time is priority #1. Sometimes we forget that.

ON MANIPULATION

IF A PERSON says "I am a master" or "I am an initiate," you can tell from the very fact that they are saying it that they aren't. And quite often what they are trying to do is manipulate people into becoming followers. That's cash flow, not spiritual growth. Don't let people elevate you to a divine status; it will mess with your mind and sooner or later you will begin to believe them. If anyone tries to kiss your foot, stand on their hand.

THE SECRETS OF LIFE

ON BEING IN FLOW

ONCE YOU are balanced and in flow and you've simplified your life, you come out of this warrior's spirit and you are not putting any negativity into your life. Then you're safe, you're abundant. You can begin to get totally in touch with who you are, and what you are is your gift to the world. You, your knowledge, your spirit, your creativity, your laughter, your positivity, the things that you have to offer—that is your gift to the world and you can charge for it. Because we're not here necessarily to give it for nothing.

THE SECRETS OF LIFE

ON FREEDOM

I F YOU are not totally free then ask yourself, why not? When did you abdicate control of your life, and if you did abdicate, did you do so voluntarily, or have you allowed someone to force it upon you?

ON DEBT

GETTING OUT of debt is vital to most, for it's hard for you to be totally free while you're in debt.
    There's a million ways of getting out of debt. *Airport* works quite well.

ON SHOPPING

ONLY THE rich can afford to go shopping in Woolworths or J.C. Penney's or K Mart. If you aren't rich, you will never become so by shopping in those places.

ON GOOD EATING

IF YOU are going to be in tune with the Universal Laws you will be living on life-giving foods. If you can't pronounce what it says on the back of a tin or packet of food, you know it can't be good for you. Life Force has easy words, like carrot.

ON DETACHMENT

S YOU become more powerful you will begin to detach from the world, for it is basically weak. Part of this detachment is your ability to withdraw from the mindset and the feelings of the society around you. Once you go beyond worrying about whether people like you or not, then you can undercut their manipulation of you and establish a feeling of total independence. As you become that powerful, independent, evolving being, you understand that you do not have to accommodate anyone, if that is not your wish.

THE SECRETS OF LIFE

ON SIMPLICITY

NCE YOU'VE taken on a metaphysics and you see yourself as infinite and you have developed some kind of creative money-making endeavor outside of tick-tock, then the final goal is to return to a simplicity of lifestyle, whereby the outer game of life (keeping it together and paying the rent), is so simple that it does not impinge on or disturb your inner spirit. Having made all these changes in your life, and having taken on new activities and a new way of looking at things, eventually you have to return to a purity of spirit, a simplicity in which you become nothing again.

ON IDENTITY

WHEN YOU can stand up and say to yourself "I am the God Force, I am God, and it is me," step #1 is complete.

ON LEAVING THINGS ALONE

IF A TREE in the forest is not perfect you don't go up to it and say "Excuse me tree but I don't really like the way you look would you mind if I lob a bit off?" You just let it be. You can't be bothered. You respect it and leave it alone. Look at all the people as if they were trees. If they ask for advice, give it. If they don't ask, walk on.

ON BEING PEACEFUL

 OU DON'T want to mess with world peace—all you want to do is be peaceful.

ON LIFE'S REFLECTION

WHAT YOU are looking at as you peer out through your eyes is a reflection of you. It is constantly you. There is nothing that you see that isn't you. If the cab driver slows down to pick you up and sees you standing there in the rain and he gives you the "up yours" sign and accelerates, that's your neat little energy that's pissed him off. He's felt your energy and voted no. As you watch the outside you're constantly watching a reflection of the inside. It is constantly teaching you about yourself.

THE SECRETS OF LIFE

ON HOW YOU FEEL ABOUT YOURSELF

I F PEOPLE are always tryin' to punch you out, you might try asking, "I wonder if my energy pattern's a bit off today? I wonder if what I feel about myself isn't quite right?"

THE SECRETS OF LIFE

ON DEATH

THE FACT is we've all bought into this thing about dying. But you say, "Everybody dies." How do you know everybody dies? Because if a person doesn't die how would you know they didn't die? Especially if you've agreed to die at a certain point in time. Right? The guy that didn't die would be livin' beyond you. So you aren't gonna be around to find out whether he died or didn't die. But we've all agreed to die. It's like a club we join. That agreement frightens you. The fact is, you agreed to it.

ON JUST BEING

THE FRUIT tree doesn't jump out of the orchard and knock on Safeway's door and say "Hey, do you need any of these?" And you too should not try and force your gifts on others. Let them know you exist and what it is that you do but wait for people to come to you. It's stronger that way. The less you appear to need people or their business, the stronger the power and eventually the greater your success.

THE SECRETS OF LIFE

THE SECRETS OF LIFE

ON TRUST

T O ALLOW yourself to be moved metaphysically you have to know and trust that all is well. To strengthen that trust within you, begin to move away from the concerns of the people. That way you will begin to believe that all is well with the world; that there is a long term plan even if we don't necessarily understand it. But more importantly than knowing and trusting that all is well with the world, you have to know and trust that all is well with you. You have to be satisfied with yourself. Because if you are dissatisfied with who you are, and if you exist in an eternal inner self, you are at this very moment eternally

THE SECRETS OF LIFE

pissed off. That's not much of an affirmation. It's like an itch you can't scratch. It will distract you from the main thrust of your desire which is to grow spiritually.

ON DISENGAGING FROM THE WORLD

NOTHING IS good or bad, cold or hot. Nothing is long or short—long in relation to what? You could walk five miles in the pouring rain and say, "This is a long journey." But is it a long journey compared to walking across the Sahara? When you disengage from the world you judge nothing. When you pull away from quantifying the world around you, you understand a great secret. You'll understand that you can just experience it as a feeling rather than as a decision or as a quantifiable something or other. Your life is an experience. It is not a high or low, failure or success-type thing. Just experience. When you treat it as

an experience you come out from the
ego and the mind into a more infinite
perception and you don't try to figure
it all out—you just concentrate on
living.   Do you understand that when
you don't say, "I like it" or "I dislike
it," that it allows you to have a more
infinite experience of whatever it is
that you are considering? When you
put it into a little box, it's over on an
energy level anyway. When you don't
quantify the experience it expands
eternally and you become more free
in your perceptions. And what
happens if you don't quantify your
life? It lays there in all its spiritual
purity, Limitless.

THE SECRETS OF LIFE

ON COMING AND GOING

THE SECRET I think to good sex is to make sure the male doesn't ejaculate too soon, so that the female can move through to a point of orgasm. Most guys can come in about 2 seconds flat—in the space of one Coca-Cola commercial, so if they're not doing their best to hang in there, the whole thing's over and done with.

THE SECRETS OF LIFE

ON SEXUALITY
SEMINARS

 USED to do sexuality lectures. It's a very hard way of making a living. Dealing with the guys is easy, you just sit around drinking beer and talk about getting laid. Everybody loves it! When you open your mouth to the females, instantly there's a hundred ferrets chewing on your nuts. I never did find out what they were all so pissed off about. Anyway, like a good little Mongol general, I have "planned retreat" as a center point in my philosophy. So much for sexuality seminars.

ON MALE SEXUALITY

YOU READ in the Taoist texts that males lose power or Chi by ejaculating. So in the olden days the monks would put jade rings on their thingies to exert control and to become, theoretically, immortal. I can understand that if you ejaculate too much, you'll tire yourself out, but I can't understand the philosophy of never ejaculating at all—that's nuts. What's the point of becoming immortal and having a crummy time getting there? It's like havin' a Ferrari in the garage and walkin' everywhere. It's stupid, isn't it?

THE SECRETS OF LIFE

ON BLUFF

I N LIFE you've gotta call everybody's bluff. And when you get really strong and secure you've got to call your own.

ON BEGINNING THINGS

 **Y**OU CAN only begin where you find yourself.

THE SECRETS OF LIFE

ON TIME

HOW MUCH time have you got? All the time in the world. Why? Because you're infinite. Remember that. Don't let life put you on the "hurry up." Repeat it three times: I have all the time in the world. I have all the time in the world. I have all the time in the world. You'll soon get it.

ON PROJECTING ENERGY

HERE ISN'T any necessity to constantly project your mind into the future. That disempowers the present. If you are putting on a picnic three Saturdays from now, you may have to do some organizational stuff today to make sure it happens. But that isn't projecting your energy forward—it's saying, "In order for us to have a picnic three Saturdays from now we need to order some picnic baskets today." The idea is to develop yourself clearly inside the present and to not pollute the future with too much thinking, so that the place where you are not (the future) is clearly defined. That helps you strengthen the present. The average person is very poorly defined because they're confused. Their energy is everywhere other than in the here and now. In polluting what is not yet real they debilitate what is real.

ON WHERE THINGS ARE NOT

HE TAOISTS taught me something neat. They showed me how to look at all of the energy of something— what it was. Then I learned to look at what it was not or where it was not. Meaning: the tree is defined by its leaves and branches but it is also defined by the sky around it (where it is not). Its boundary. Where does this thing end? That helps you identify what it is. Then when you look in the same way at your life you can see what is real, what is there, and you can also think about what is not there, right now. That helps you identify what you are. It helps you become real. It allows you to strengthen yourself by living in the truth.

THE SECRETS OF LIFE

I N METAPHYSICS we look at the antithesis of things. The opposite. And as you begin to look at things more and more from a metaphysical viewpoint, you see the opposite as being a vital part. The antithesis is as important as what is.

ON THE ANTITHESIS OF THINGS

THERE IS an antithesis in life that actually complements what you are and you can use it. It's like the shadow in the light. You can't have light without a darkness in which it will shine. So you have to honor the darkness that assists the light in becoming something. That's why I don't have much time for those woolly-headed characters who say that the world ought to be all cozy and lovely and guaranteed. That Utopian love-fest is not going to happen, for if it did, all the human spirits evolving through the earthplane would suddenly head off. There would be no challenge. We would all return to the spirit world where the love-fest is a lot better. You can't have courage unless there is weakness. You can't have goodness unless there's a notion of evil. And you can't have spiritual growth unless there is something for you to knock up against. You should thank God that things aren't perfect.

ON DON'T LET THE SUCKERS
GRIND YOU DOWN

YOU'VE ALWAYS gotta call everybody's bluff. Ninety-nine times out of a hundred—call their bluff and you'll get away with it. If they try to maneuver you—call 'em. When they say, "If you don't do this and that you're gonna be outta this job," answer, "Fine. Here's the key to the executive restroom—eat it." If you always call their bluff nobody can maneuver you because you're strong. Why? Because you're not coming out of lack and fear, like, this is the only job in the world. You're not coming out of survival, or there isn't enough to go 'round. You're not coming out of "there's a rush." You've got all the time in the world. All possibilities are open to

THE SECRETS OF LIFE

you. Don't let people manipulate you by trying to play on survival issues. Stay on the high ground. Don't let the suckers grind you down.

ON NEGOTIATING

 KNOW that the win-win philosophy in negotiating is very popular nowadays. But that's not Mongolian. That's pathetic. You're not here to keep everybody happy. Most of you have been doing that for too long. You are here to master life and to make it simple and quick for yourself. So when someone says, "How much do you want?" You reply, "All of it." It's a great place to start, isn't it? If they say, "What about win-win?" you say, "Here's a deal. Under the laws of win-win you'd be happy with 50% right. OK, let's do this: you take 25% less than what you want and I'll take 25% less than what I want. That's win-win. We'll both reduce our expectations by

THE SECRETS OF LIFE

25%." A lot of you have got out there; you're bright-eyed and bushy-tailed, you put it together, but forgot to ask for what you wanted, or, you devalued what you wanted. The name of the game is to ask for what you want. Start with "all of it" and work back from there. It's a good exercise in assertiveness.

ON YOUR WORD AS LAW

HE WORDS you use are important, for your mind is used to you giving it your impressions, your assessments. You are the general and your mind is the foot soldier. If you say, "It's hard," the mind believes that and creates the circumstances "hard" to fit the opinion you have given it. If you say, "It's simple—it's bloody simple," that's how it will be. You decide. Your words are important. If you constantly moan that life's a pain in the butt, you'll one day wake up with piles.

THE SECRETS OF LIFE

ON NURTURING YOURSELF

UR LIVES are designed around sustaining a whole something. The more stuff you have to sustain the more complicated your life becomes. Then you find that your life is no longer designed around your pleasure, your energy, or your nurturing. Instead it is a welfare office that you sustain, finance and manage for others. What is the point of that? You have to nurture yourself and take care of your needs first.

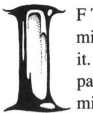

ON THE GOVERNMENT'S LARGESSE

IF THE government makes a mistake, you get to pay for it. If there's a disaster, you pay for it, even though you might have worked hard to keep your life in balance. If the politicians decide to send three billion dollars to some obscure place in order to win the local vote back home, you get to pay for their largesse. All this can get on your nerves. But once you realize that the system of power is not designed to nurture or benefit you, you can concentrate on working upon yourself and develop a consciousness outside the evolution of tick-tock, and at that point you don't give a damn who's getting the money and who isn't. You just incorporate enough bigness and abundance to include all

THE SECRETS OF LIFE

the loo-loo things the government is
going to bill you for.

ON FLAKY GOVERNMENTS

LL OF the governments have let all of the people down, all of the time. Once you understand that, you can stop wondering what the hell they are going to do next and get on with your life.

ON THE SENSUALITY OF LIFE

ABUNDANCE IS an appreciation for life, its sensuality. It is the appreciation for the fine things in life—like the beauty of a flower, a swim in a cold lake on a hot day. Abundance is a whole gamut of things, one's friendships, one's relationships, one's experience of life. Many live in prison cells of sensual poverty—they don't open their hearts to the sensuality of life and accept its gifts.

THE SECRETS OF LIFE

ON LIFE'S BANQUET

WHAT'S THE point of being invited to this incredible banquet of life, if you're so wrapped up in being at the banquet that you forget to eat?

THE SECRETS OF LIFE

ON PRIDE

RIDE THAT you express to other people is ego. Pride that you express silently to yourself is real pride. Pride of self is understanding that life is glorious, and that it is an honor to be here. Appreciate what you are and accept that.

ON FEMININITY

 T IS important that the female develops a reality that honors and nurtures her femininity and has an identity and creativity of her own. It is equally important that the male in the relationship endorses that creativity.

ON FEMININE SOFTNESS

WHAT MAKES a woman beautiful is the softness she exudes. It isn't a physical beauty. It's an inner softness, the warmth, the purity, the caring, the nurturing. It's not the shape of her body or the shape of her face. Many women who have beautiful faces have revolting energy.

THE SECRETS OF LIFE

ON MASCULINE POWER

MALES UNDERSTAND power by doing things that are powerful. Women just understand power.

THE SECRETS OF LIFE

ON SACRIFICE

SACRIFICE IS a manifestation of the ego. If I spend all day washin' socks, will you love me? The Life Force doesn't ask you to be a martyr and wash socks all day long. You can either wash 'em or not wash 'em. If you don't wash 'em, he'll just have to buy some more.

ON CONFIDENCE

TEP ACROSS the line—believe in yourself. Agree to be right. Even when you are wrong. In an eternal sense there is only one category: "Right."

ON SIMPLIFYING YOUR LIFE

OOK AT having a spotless existence. Walk in trust that all will be OK. Simplicity must be there in your life. The Living Spirit does not have anger. The Living Spirit does not worry about how to pay the rent. Simplify. Bring up the balance. Make the outer game so simple that it does not impinge or infringe on the inner you. Stay on the path that has the least resistance. Allow your inner life to catch up. You will have an infinity, a stronger power and knowledge that is the natural state of being within. Simplicity is the state of becoming nothing again.

ON ACQUIRING KNOWLEDGE

METAPHYSICS IS knowing that you know everything. It is knowing that you know nothing. It's knowing that you are happy with that.

ON BECOMING IMPECCABLE

BECOME MORE of the infinite God Force within you. Be immaculate. Be impeccable. Have little or no unfinished business. Make each step impeccable. Focus. Use up as little as possible. Disturb nothing. Clean up your life. Tie up the loose ends.

THE SECRETS OF LIFE

ON SERENITY

YIN IS a composed serenity, a sense of self-identity. It is a belief in self. It is the God Force within all things. Identify with that yin in all things. Your composure keeps you safe. Nothing should be allowed to destroy that serenity. Serenity comes with softness. It comes through your dominating your life. Touch it. Hold it. Let it shine silently from your heart.

ON INDIVIDUALITY IN RELATIONSHIPS

 **Y**OU MUST understand that the person you choose to be with is an individual. They can never be you and you can never be them. You honor that individuality in them and you honor yourself. That understanding should be sacrosanct. Then the relationship that develops escalates into an incredible crescendo of energy.

ON THE ETERNAL TAO

ECOME THE Tao! Be like nature, big in your feelings. Then you can love everything because once you become larger than life you can then incorporate all of it in your heart.

ON FEMALE SUPPORT

F THE female will subjugate her ego and support the male unequivocally, what happens is the male goes beyond his identity crisis and he begins to understand himself. The energy he projects will then become stronger. He pulls more money and the family gradually becomes stronger. But it is difficult for the female to subjugate her ego, for that requires a very spiritual approach. If she can do it, it will work real well. If she can't there are other ways.

ON SPIRITUAL GROWTH

N THE land of the spiritually blind the one-eyed man is king, even if he is wearing a contact lens. Any progress is encouraging.

ON THE WEALTH
OF THE NATION

HE WEALTH of the nation is the individual man, the individual woman, the working people of the country. We create the wealth and the government gets to play with the proceeds of our energy. They get to spend your cash pretty much anyway they like. There's no point in getting pissed off—ignore them. Hopefully, they'll go away.

THE SECRETS OF LIFE

ON BANKS

HAVE never been very keen on banks. It's not polite to ask that many personal questions. Plus, they have a way of making you wrong all of the time. When you have loads of cash in the bank they don't thank you and when you screw up they pounce on you like you're a Commie and a rat. It's not your fault you can't count. Let's face it, if you could count what the hell would you need the bloody bank for?

ON SEEING BEAUTY

THE WAY to motivate yourself is to constantly see the utter beauty in all things. There's beauty even in ugliness. Anyone can look at a rose and call it beautiful but try seeing beauty in a friend who's deliberately ripping you off— that's harder.

ON KNOCKIN' YOURSELF OUT

 F YOU'RE knockin' yourself out, struggling like crazy, what you're sayin' is, "I don't know what I'm doing, and I'm too stupid or idle to change it."

THE SECRETS OF LIFE

ON ORGANIZING YOUR TIME

HE WAY to control your life is to control your time frames. If you don't have enough time, it says, "You're out of control." Analyze what is important in your life, keep the best, bag the rest.

ON FLUIDITY

MANY OF you are overweight...in things. And whereas at the beginning, things gave you pleasure—in the end they don't anymore. They drain you because you've got to look after them. You've got to service them, protect them, polish them. That's why I dislike cars because you have to look after the bloody things. I wish we had disposable ones—like Kleenex. You know, every Thursday or Saturday you'd truck it someplace and trash it and they'd give you another one.

THE SECRETS OF LIFE

THE SECRETS OF LIFE

ON INTENTION

LL THERE is to say about dedication is you will not meet one person in a hundred who is dedicated. Will you? And all you've got to do is agree to be dedicated. And that means you lock on like a missile to the intention that you have for your life. What do you want? Demand that life give it to you. Half the problem that some of you have had in the past is that you are too wimpy about demanding what it is you want. And isn't it true that we have a tendency to think that other people know what we want? They don't. And they don't care, until you tell them. If you walk up to people and tell 'em what you want, they may not necessarily give you what you want, but at least you've expressed your intention. Your word is law. Go tell the world what you want. How much do you want? All of it! Right?

ON ACHIEVING YOUR GOALS

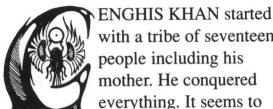ENGHIS KHAN started with a tribe of seventeen people including his mother. He conquered everything. It seems to me you don't need much in life other than enthusiasm and your mum.

ON WINNERS

WHEN PEOPLE ask me what football team I support, I say, "I support the team that's on top that's doing well." I can't support a club if its record is 0 and 11. Losers bother me. They ought to bother you.

THE SECRETS OF LIFE

ON DEVELOPING PLANS

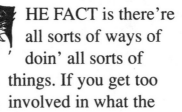

THE FACT is there're all sorts of ways of doin' all sorts of things. If you get too involved in what the other people say can and can't be done, you tend to lose the focus of your plan. It's better therefore that you work on your plan silently without discussing it with others, except when you have to.

ON CONFUSION

F YOU'VE ever been confused, I can fix it for you in one minute flat. But you have to agree to follow my instructions to the letter. The way to get rid of confusion is to agree to never ask any questions. You can't be confused unless you ask questions. Don't ask.

ON PERPETUAL JOY

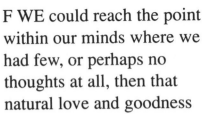

F WE could reach the point within our minds where we had few, or perhaps no thoughts at all, then that natural love and goodness that comes up from our hearts, the connection we have with all things, would spring forth and we would enter a state of perpetual joy.

ON MARRIAGE

I N MARRIAGE or in any relationship, you have to learn to communicate. What's fun about relationships is that the other person reflects back to you who you are. When you're married, your spouse tends to let you know of your shortcomings extremely quickly, like in about two minutes flat. So you learn about yourself and begin to see yourself in a new light.

ON YOUNG CHILDREN

THE WAY to help children is to allow them to be who they are. It's helpful to remember they are grown-up spirits in little bodies. It is also important to remember that the child's spirit (its Higher Self) has a certain characteristic that will draw the child gradually into various experiences in life, that will materialize either in the positive or the negative depending on the individual's focus. There is nothing much you can do about the eventual direction the child will take. All you can do is give it the best tools possible for handling life and to applaud when the child does well and to be there for it when it falls on its face.

THE SECRETS OF LIFE

ON FAMILY LIFE

NE OF the things I like about family life is that you get to bitch and argue with people who you know, in the comfort of your own home.

ON THE NATURALNESS OF KIDS

**Y**OU LEARN a lot from kids—they are so natural. It's amazing that we grown-ups forget so quickly how easy naturalness is. Let's face it, it wasn't that many years ago that we stood with a group of people in the drawing room and pee'd on the carpet without so much of an "if you please," or "do you mind."

ON CHANCE

T IS said that you should never leave anything to chance. But in operating like that, chance never leaves anything to you.

ON THE DESTINY OF THE WORLD

I FIRMLY believe the world will sort itself out in the end. Believe it with me. At least none of us will be around to be proven wrong.

ON OVER-WORKING

FOR YEARS I was a workaholic. Then one day I changed my mind. Now I am self-unemployed. I like it better that way.

ON FINANCIAL ENLIGHTENMENT

PEOPLE SOONER or later realize that in order to be free, you have to have money. If you don't concentrate on money, you'll never have any. And if you don't have any, it's difficult to be truly free. I'm not saying you can't join a Buddhist monastery someplace and just have your little bowl and a grain of rice that you chase with a chopstick for four hours and then 'ol Zendo Bendo comes along and thwacks you over the ear with a stick and you touch nirvana. That's one way. But somehow I think my way is more pleasing.

THE SECRETS OF LIFE

ON AWARENESS

PERSON WHO is not aware, who will not open to new perceptions, basically walks in a concrete overcoat. It's hard to operate through life like that. You have to be open to change and new ideas. Even if that is a little threatening. Even if it means that something or someone will come along and turn all of your sacred cows into dog meat.

ON PERSONAL ENLIGHTENMENT

FALLING IN love with yourself, not in an egocentric sense, but falling in love because you've forgiven yourself, you appreciate yourself. Knowing that you are this carefree scamp allows you to fall in love with life, and you can see a laughter, a silliness, a beauty in all things. You can see the courage that is naturally in your heart. And you can watch that courage walk out into life and demonstrate your mastery over it. Gradually, that mastery will grant you enlightenment.

THE SECRETS OF LIFE

THE SECRETS OF LIFE

ON EMOTIONAL DISCIPLINE

EMOTIONAL DISCIPLINE is not not having emotions. It is more a matter of not allowing them to run amok all over your life without your taking a look at them. "Hey, why am I upset?" "Why am I angry?" "Why am I stabbin' the cat with this hair drier?" Stuff like that.

THE SECRETS OF LIFE

ON OVERSTIMULATION

THE PROBLEM with the constant stimulation of modern life is that you gradually become numb to it and so you have to create more and more stimulation in order for it to have any effect. So what we find is that sooner or later, we are cramming our day full of stuff in order to get over the anguish we feel because the day is crammed full of stuff.

ON DISADVANTAGES

HERE WAS a young man once who had been born with a defect. One of his legs was much shorter than the other. His lack of mobility bothered him greatly. So he climbed up a mountain to visit a great sage who was reputed to live high in the valleys. He literally crawled and pulled himself up that mountain for days until he finally came upon the sage. He asked, "Sir, I was born with this defect and one of my legs is much shorter than the other. What should I do?" The sage paused in silence for a moment and then said, "Limp." The young man got it. He went off and became a great healer.

THE SECRETS OF LIFE

ON TRAVELING

 HAVE traveled constantly all my life. Wanderlust must have been in my veins at birth. I don't know about you but I find I use places up. When you first go to a place it seems magical and interesting and everything is new and fresh and it exhilarates you. Then one morning you wake up and the cute little store on the corner is not so cute and a cockroach walks across your plate at the little bistro you so loved. All the people you see tell you all the things they told you last week, and suddenly you realize that you've drained the place of the magic it held for you. At that point my mind begins a faint hum. It's unintelligible at first, but as

THE SECRETS OF LIFE

I listen carefully I can hear it getting louder and louder and I realize it's saying to me, "Airport! Airport! Airport!"

THE SECRETS OF LIFE

ON LETTING GO

OFTEN, IN order to find yourself you have to be prepared to let go. That can make you insecure. It is as if you are forced to lose yourself and many of those facets of your personality that you hold so dear, in order for you to quiet the mind and return gradually back to the source. Whereupon you discover yourself again.

ON PERFECTION

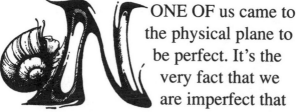

ONE OF us came to the physical plane to be perfect. It's the very fact that we are imperfect that makes this whole spiritual quest so bloody marvelous. That imperfection allows you to develop a forgiveness in your heart. Not only forgiveness of yourself, but a forgiveness that you offer others. You can cut them a little slack, Jack. You don't have to push people to be perfect. And as you grant that forgiveness to yourself, others in turn grant you more leeway and soon you begin to see how beautifully bizarre life is.

ON CONTROLLING PEOPLE THROUGH LENDING

DEBT IS how the status quo controls the common people. You can have all the rules and regulations you want, you can build massive police forces and tax systems, but debt is the easiest way of controlling the population and those who have power over us know that. That is why they make debt so easy to assume. When the Western world gave up its empires, all it did was lend the lesser developed countries plenty of money and 'hey presto,' all the control mechanisms were still there. Don't get suckered in. If you are in debt, work on a plan to get out. Being debt-free is the common man's way of saying "up yours" to the system.

THE SECRETS OF LIFE

# ON PERSONAL DEBT

IN ATTEMPTING to materialize our hopes and dreams we often commit to great amounts of personal debt. Yet that debt often is our way of replacing creativity and effort with other people's money. We tend to think that the only way a project will come off is to go borrow three quarters of a million. What I found was that I used debt as a stopgap. It's easier to borrow a bunch of money than to think up ways of materializing the project with what one has at hand, or by borrowing a lot less. It seemed to me that I used debt instead of creative cleverness. The debt blocked me from getting the money by other ways, or it blocked me from perhaps making the project

THE SECRETS OF LIFE

happen in a smaller way but in a way that had integrity and possibilities rather than being lumbered down by commitment. So one day I banned myself from all debt. It took me three years to pay everything off, but by forcing myself to operate on a cash basis I stimulated my financial power and everything came together stronger and more solid than ever before. There was a horrible period at the beginning where I went through withdrawal symptoms, but I soon got over that. The power I felt from operating in the now with what was financially real more than compensated. The end result was that in a thousand days I turned several hundreds of thousands of debt into the exact same figure of cash credit. I never looked back and I never took on any more debt.

ON LOVE

MOST PEOPLE express love emotionally and that comes off like "a wet lick in the ear." Love is a settled heart, a big heart—love is having the compassion to leave things alone.

ON SEX AND IMMORTALITY

S A YOUNG man I read all those Taoist and Hindu texts that show you how to raise the sexual kundalini from the root chakra to the crown and become immortal. I spent a number of happy years working on it. Then suddenly it struck me that if there was one thing that all those Taoists and Hindu immortals had in common, it was that they were all extremely dead. Oh well, you win a few and you lose a few.

ON MAKING THINGS SPECIAL

WHAT IS real is what you have here right now. If you can make what you have special, then every moment of every day becomes special. If you constantly project forward to the future or to things that may or may not come about, you devalue what it is that you have created. In devaluing what is real, you also pull energy away from your hopes and dreams and when they do finally show up you'll devalue them. So it's dumb to ignore the present in favor of a possible future which, when finally materialized, will disappoint you. It's better that you energize the present with your approval.

THE SECRETS OF LIFE

ON LIPS

LIPS ARE handy, they stop your mouth from fraying. You can learn a lot about people by looking at their lips. It's as if the central statement of a person's life is gradually etched on their lips thereby changing their shape to accommodate whatever is being said.

ON PEOPLE

NE OF the things I like about humanity is that there's lots of it. It would be a hell of a drag if you had to wander around for days just to find someone to talk to.

ON THE TOOTH FAIRY

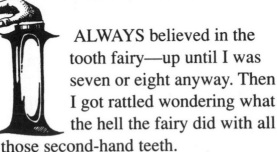

ALWAYS believed in the tooth fairy—up until I was seven or eight anyway. Then I got rattled wondering what the hell the fairy did with all those second-hand teeth.

ON MEN IN BROWN POLYESTER SUITS

EWARE OF men in brown polyester suits. They'll either try to hug you or sell you something.

ON NEGATIVITY

IF THROUGH insecurity you perpetually concentrate on misfortune, that act of concentration draws to you the very things you've been hoping to avoid. It comes along and bites you on the bum. It finds you. In fact it will cross town to get you.

ON DEMOCRACY FOR THE ENLIGHTENED

UNFORTUNATELY THERE is no such thing as democracy for the enlightened. With a system based on one man-one vote, you are bound to have a social disorder designed to pander to the survival fears and tribal psychosis of the masses. By becoming somewhat enlightened you will always be slightly odd, a bit of a weirdo because you've gone beyond the petty neuroses of the collective mind-set. You have to accept that you will never fit anymore. You become what I call a "fringe-dweller." Don't fight it, there're millions of us.

THE SECRETS OF LIFE

ON LEARNING
THROUGH MISTAKES

WE CAME to this earthplane without a manual. We're not a Japanese digital box complete with instructions in nine languages. We just plopped here and we have to muddle along tryin' to understand what the hell's going on without anyone really showin' us, "Hey, this is the way." And so if you allow the guilt trips of life to mess with you, it will rot your brain. The mistakes you made—you needed them. And the people you impacted through those mistakes—they needed them also. And so bit by bit, realizing that, you can come to a healing of your life.

THE SECRETS OF LIFE

ON REGIMEN

THERE IS a big difference between regimen and discipline. Regimen is a system for the simple-minded. You might need discipline, but if you are a carefree scamp, why do you need regimen?

ON KNIGHTS IN ARMOR

S YOUNG girls, females are taught to defend and preserve their sexuality, and quite rightly so. The problem is that defense becomes a programmed response. So eventually when their knight in shining armor does show up they give him a hard time also. He stands outside the walls in the pouring rain wondering what the hell he's supposed to do next. And rather than letting the draw bridge down and opening the gates, the female makes the sucker swim the moat, climb the ivy and clamber up the hard way. It's not surprising that when he gets through all that, he is so wasted that the whole performance turns out a bit of a flop. It seems to

THE SECRETS OF LIFE

me there ought to be a middle ground
between not acting like a slut, and
giving your sucker an even break.

ON SEXUALITY

NE OF the main problems with sexuality is that it makes a lot of people nervous. Possibly because most haven't been laid since the ol' king died.

ON THE ILLOGICAL

BEYOND LOGIC and facts and all of man's accumulated scientific knowledge, there is the power of spirit which is often illogical. Things happen that are wonderful and unexpected and that come from nowhere and it's pointless to try to work them out. Understand that they are manifestations of your energy—the outward expressions of your feelings that you get to experience and enjoy. It is energy or spirit responding to what you are and what you have become. Who needs logic to be a part of that? You just need energy.

THE SECRETS OF LIFE

ON ACCEPTING RESPONSIBILITY

NCE YOU accept that the world is basically beautiful and that you are one hundred percent responsible for your evolution, you understand that if something jumps out of the sidewalk and bites you on the bum, it's a manifestation of your energy. You also understand that life is a teaching symbol of the quality of the inner you. So if you need to know, "How am I doing?," look around you. Every second of every moment of the day the Great Spirit is giving you a print-out of how things are going. So if someone comes up to you and says, "How wonderful to see you, it's just so neat. Could you look after this $5000 for me? I'm going to Australia to marry a young woman. I'll be back in forty years," you know things are moving in the right direction.

ON SEEKING RECOGNITION

S YOUR energy grows and you work upon yourself, people will be pulled to you and you will wind up helping them. There is a point on the journey where one tends to seek some kind of recognition from the inner light for the work one has done. But you will be disappointed to discover that the inner dimensions are devoid of thanks and recognition. Blank, nothing, nixy-dixy. In the early days that used to bug me. Then I realized that it's only one's ego that needs the recognition and the thanks and that the part of you that actually did the work—spirit—does not need to thank itself.

THE SECRETS OF LIFE

 ON CHASING MONEY

I LIKE money. I always have. But you have to stalk it, to woo it. It's like a skittish girlfriend who is constantly trying to tow you around by the nose, dancing with all the other blokes. The more you chase her the more she drives you nuts. But sit in the corner and jangle the car keys and she'll come home with you, because she's not up for walking.

ON MONEY, EMOTION AND SECURITY

O THE man in the street money is the God Force. It is the one thing that allows him to feel a sense of security and a sense of purpose. Through money he experiences the ability to control his life. Because it is such a symbol of status and security, it is natural therefore that money and emotion go hand-in-hand. That's why everybody's tearing around like chickens with their heads cut off trying to get it. However, the more you surround your money-making ventures with emotion and insecurity, the less money you will have. That explains why most people don't have any real money to speak of, in spite of going bonkers fifteen hours a day for

THE SECRETS OF LIFE

years, trying to acquire it. Once you "click" your mind from money-equals-security, to money-equals-creative freedom, then your emotions relax and you don't have to chase money 'round and 'round like an idiot. It will just jump in your lap. You'll like that a lot better.

ON SERVICE

THE SECRET to service is your ability to subjugate your ego to the buyer's needs long enough to take his money. If you subjugate your ego to serve the customer, they feel that service, but moreover they feel your support. Then they don't care so much what the price is. To serve successfully you have to be able to put yourself underneath the customer and not allow your ego to get in the way. Say you're working in a bar. When a person comes into your bar, what they're basically doing is escaping momentarily from the terror of daily life. Most people out there in tick-tock are living in various states of unholy terror. They live in dysfunctional relationships and they work for manipulative companies. Those people are scared. Everyone is scared to a lesser or greater degree. Once you understand that they are bringing this unholy terror into your bar, all you have to do is play doctor and nurse. So, if you are in a position where you are serving people, all you have to put across is: There isn't any limit to what I will do to fix your life for you. I'm doing it, not because you're going to tip me, but because you've honored me by bringing your dis-ease into my bar, and I am going to heal your fear for you temporarily. Once you know how to give off that "Come here and let Mummy kiss it better" energy, money starts to find you at high speed.

ON THE PSYCHOLOGY OF SELLING

MONEY IS so inexorably linked to security in the mind of the common man. It is vitally important to remember that when you are trying to sell him something. In order for him to transfer his money to you he has to feel safe. The easiest way to make him feel safe is to get underneath him psychologically and really act out of love and support. You have to take the buyer past whatever survival considerations he might have. You do this by clearly defining the benefit of the item or service you are selling, by reassuring him that he is safe, that the world is OK and that things will last forever. That's what he wants to hear.

THE SECRETS OF LIFE

So tell him that. If you both believe
it, it will help make that a reality.
Why not?

ON AGREEING TO BE RICH

ONCE YOU feel strong about yourself, all of a sudden money flows and all you are looking to do is to go beyond the emotion surrounding money and to open the faucet. The wealth of the world is so fantastic that if you divided it up among the people equally, everyone would be a millionaire. So our natural state is to be millionaires. Anything less is either where you have found yourself by birth or where you have put yourself through time. Poverty in the western world is unnatural. Once you agree that your natural state is to be rich, wealth starts to find you. Change your mind. Let's go shopping!

THE SECRETS OF LIFE

ON SELLING
PEOPLE THINGS

A S YOU begin to go out into the marketplace and begin to seek out people, you expand. As your energy rises, people will be attracted to you. At that point you will have to think in terms of what you are going to sell'em when they show up. There are only three things that people buy: a knowledge, a service, or a product. There is nothing else people want. So you have to think of what it is that you will offer the world. Once you have made your decision, then work on imbuing your offering with energy. Make it bright and light, make it informative, make it useful, and if you can, try to go up-market. There is not a lot of pleasure in selling little plastic diddlies made in Taiwan.

ON CREATIVITY

CREATIVITY IS one of the greatest expressions of the God Force on the physical plane. It's a test isn't it, to go past the awkwardness we feel in creating things and to create them anyway. It's fine to create things for your own pleasure, but the quintessence of creativity is doing something that you love to do and getting paid for it. How much more brilliant can you get? It's not work, is it? The problem arises when you have to present your creativity to the marketplace and face the possibilities of rejection. Fear sets in and the mind can suck you into all sorts of ego-oriented opinions that keep you poor. So much of the snobbery surrounding

THE SECRETS OF LIFE

art is a by-product of the artist's ego and fear. Rather than creating something people will buy, the artist waxes lyrical about not wanting to besmirch the purity of his or her art by adjusting to commercial reality. But the reality is that if the public won't buy a cow turd nailed to a canvas, it's not their fault. The fault lies in the artist's mediocrity or his or her lack of perception, not the taste of the buying public. So if you have to adjust somewhat to make it work, I suggest you compromise and pay the rent.

ON NEGATIVE YEARNING

DON'T YEARN for things you haven't got. The emotion of yearning creates a powerful negative affirmation inside you that literally pushes the thing you desire away from you. Why is that? Because through negative yearning you devalue the power of the present— what is real right now. Then your ability to materialize your dreams is lessened because your current energy is lowered by your negativity. If you want a Porsche don't pine. Say to yourself, "I want that car. I know I can have it, for in my heart I feel it is already a part of my life. Meanwhile, I am happy driving this 'ol banger for it feels like a Porsche to me."

THE SECRETS OF LIFE

ON STAYING BALANCED

IN AMERICA it costs you $750.00 just to walk through the door of a hospital, so you are forced to stay balanced and to care for yourself. Your whole body says, "Forget it, we can't afford to get sick." Then if you look at other countries that have socialized free medicine like the British National Health System, you can see how ill-health is a way of life there. If your body conks out you just haul it 'round to the Government and they'll fix it for free. There is no incentive to stay balanced and to choose a healthy way of life. Free medicine seems to make you sick. That doesn't make any sense to me.

ON BEING SELF-MOTIVATED

SELF-MOTIVATION GOES back to intent, courage, determination, and finally the sense of "I am what I am" sort of acceptance. In our society we don't teach our children warriorhood. We teach them to become what I call kings and queens of Wimpendom. They rule over nothing in particular, least of all themselves. Our incredibly vapid, bland societies are built on junk food, television, and titillation, because people do not grant empowerment to themselves. There's no charismatic spirit to sustain them. The immediacy of metaphysical reality is what grants one excitement. Animals stay extremely tuned with their

THE SECRETS OF LIFE

surroundings because they are both the hunter and the hunted. In western civilized democracies we're so comfortable, closeted and coddled. Things are so vapid. There's a safety net that makes everything guaranteed and safe. If you fall below a certain level the great paramedic in the sky comes and gives you food stamps or something. If we cut all that out and there was a psychic immediacy to survival, then everybody would get charismatically involved. You can see this confirmed in history. A country like England needs a war every so often just to keep its adrenals going.

ON COLLECTING
EXPERIENCES

THE WARRIOR understands that to go beyond the earth plane he or she will have to collect experiences. By experiencing life, you become familiar with it; by becoming familiar with it, you go beyond fear.

ON SERVING THE WORLD

SERVICE IN its true purity is only the custodianship of the energy within you. You serve by the sustained elevated energy of the warrior's quest and you serve in the very act of being here in the physical. Life in itself is a dedication into service, for you have agreed to depart from your abode of light just to be here.

ON TRANSCENDING FEAR

ECAUSE I teach seminars on facing fear, I naturally have thought a lot about how we as humans transcend fear. The conclusion I came to was that we can't completely eliminate fear for we can never know everything. So the name of the game is to transmute fear from a paralyzing force into a motivating force rather than wasting time trying to suppress it or transcend it. A small percentage of your fears are real and should be respected. They are valuable. They keep you safe and motivate you into action. But the vast majority of your fears are just negative dialogue that dribbles from the mind. The way to work with that is to begin to talk to

the fear as if it were another person.
So you say, "Thank you, I appreciate
that possibility you have just offered
me. However, given the current
circumstances of my life, I do not
accept that negative possibility as a
reality in my life. Further, the idea
of my being eaten by a wild animal
here at the bus station is a little
remote. But thank you anyway and
ciao, baby."

ON HOPE AND COURAGE

F YOU believe and trust in the God Force, it sustains you. You may not understand how it operates in your life, but it is there and all will come to pass and there will be balance in the end. So you should never give up hope. Even if you can't see how things will turn out, just continue to know and believe that the Force is with you and the outcome will be the best possible given the circumstances. Tenacity allows you to hold on long enough for the Universe to deliver to you a solution. You concentrate on the major things and allow the God Force to figure out the details. Courage, dear friend, courage. Once you feel you are truly a part of the God Force,

THE SECRETS OF LIFE

nothing is ever lost, for God cannot lose itself. All negativity is transmuted to goodness and light in the end.

ON ETERNAL LOVE

N THE eternity of things, love is not an emotion. It is respecting others—allowing them to be whatever they wish to be. Even if what they are might seem to us as evil. The greatest love you can express is not to judge others but to surrender and allow them the time to come to correct solutions on their own. For within man there is a long forgotten dream; a dream in which we remember our true heritage in the abode of light, and that we are truly infinite.

ON GAYS

I HAVE never quite understood why society discriminates against gay men and women. Why should a person's sexual preference be of any concern to others? If a gay couple treat each other with kindness and respect and they love each other, that surely adds to the goodness in the world. Love is love, whether it is mother and child, female with female or friend with friend. You can't stick love and its physical expression, sex, into a little box and say we will only approve of love if and when it is expressed under circumstances that we consider acceptable. In a world where there is so much grotty energy, any expression of love should be encouraged and applauded.

THE SECRETS OF LIFE

ON
WIMPY PEOPLE

MANY PEOPLE are wimps. Lovely, but wimpy. You can love them, hug them, give them a donut. But, they're no bloody use. That's encouraging. You don't have to elevate yourself very far in order to make it in life. I like that. It spurs me on.

THE SECRETS OF LIFE

ON STRESS CONTROL

HERE ARE all sorts of handy techniques offered nowadays to busy executives to help them manage stress in their lives. Here's my technique: retire early—like, yesterday.

ON NEW AGE PHILOSOPHIES

FTEN WHAT the New Age created were warriors of the "soggy Kleenex" variety, people just as weak as those left behind. In the cult of the Warrior-Sage is a new form of spirituality based on naturalness, truth and an unpretentious lifestyle. The Warrior, detached as he is from his death, is not looking to survive. He concentrates instead on living, experiencing each moment to the fullest, knowing it may be his last. He accepts circumstances as they come even if they may be uncomfortable, dangerous and uncertain. He realizes that many of the mysteries of life will always remain hidden so he settles comfortably into "not-knowing" and

THE SECRETS OF LIFE

turns his attention from pondering the future into concentrating on the present and whatever he finds in front of him. Dedication is the Warrior's prayer unto himself. All you can offer the world is your strength, your honor, and the quality of your quest exemplified by your life. In the next decade you will see the mechanical world of tick-tock unravel as never before. If you give your power away to institutions, circumstances will eat your lunch. If you step inside the Warrior-Sage philosophy you are left with just yourself, but at least you are left with a person you can trust.

ON THE UNGLUING

THE WORLD is sort of ungluing. The emotional base of the people is weaker now. Many are hypnotized by the glitter that is outside of them. It is as if the building is burning, and they just keep turning the music up louder so the roar of the flames cannot be heard. The sensible ones are taking note of conditions and walking slowly to the fire escape before it's too late.

THE SECRETS OF LIFE

ON SOCIETY AND DRUGS

THE REASON society doesn't like the drug industry is because all the dopers remind society of all the stuff it's also hooked on. In the U.S. we consume seventy million Valium tablets every day. Add to that all the other tranquilizers, uppers, downers, sleepers and booze, and what we have is a society that's mostly stoned out of its brain all of the time. I love it when a row of those podgy ladies from middle America get up on the Oprah Winfrey Show, and waffle on about how rotten the druggies are. Meanwhile, all those wholesome ladies are doped up to the eyeballs. If you want to fix drugs you are going to have to fix society first. Secondly, you are going to have to wean everyone off their addictions. I am damn glad that's not my job.

ON FIXING THE DRUG PROBLEM

MOST OF the world's problems are easily fixable, but it's not the problems that bother people, it's the solutions. Take drugs. If I were President, I'd fix the whole mess overnight by making drugs legal. I would create a taxed government monopoly on the processing and distributing of drugs and I would impose the death penalty on anyone else trying to get into the business. Next, I would treat drug addiction as a disease, which it is, rather than a criminal act. I would put back into society the taxes raised and the money saved on policing, and build treatment centers for the dopers. Meanwhile, I'd give hard drugs away

THE SECRETS OF LIFE

free, which is a lot cheaper than the price we pay right now with all the rip-offs the dopers have to commit to stay sane. The problem is that too many of the high-up people (not to mention the cops) are making too much money out of the dope business. Also the government doesn't like to face the voting public by admitting that dope is a fact of life and we will have to legalize it if we want to fix it.

ON BUSY WORK

I F YOU analyze your life you will probably find that much of the effort you put in gets you little or no return. The mind creates for you "busy work," which is nothing more than rushing around without a definite plan or direction, killing time till the day ends. As you become centered on who you are and what you want, the effort you put into your life begins to pay dividends. You telescope the amount of time you need to finish a project into tighter and tighter packets of concerted action. By identifying which of your actions bring rewards and which do not, you eliminate the dross and make way for simplicity and success. Ideally, your life should

THE SECRETS OF LIFE

be designed so that your needs come to you rather than you having to chase after them. By being organized and disciplined you will tend to hit the bull's-eye with just one dart. That leaves you time to eat chocolate and go fishing!

ON MINORITIES AND THE IMPARTIALITY OF THE GOD FORCE

I'M NOT keen on all this stuff about the underprivileged minorities. For even though the disadvantage of the minorities in society is very real to them, the God Force doesn't know whether you are black, brown, pink, turquoise or green. It does not have any judgement or opinions about you. So, anybody can make it if they will stop moaning and put in a little effort. As you pull out of the emotion that says, "I am so dis-advantaged, ain't that awful," and you concentrate instead on "making it" in life—then you make it.

THE SECRETS OF LIFE

ON LIVING YOUR DESTINY

 OU LIVE your own destiny. Nothing forces or manipulates you or makes you be something else. The God Force does not ask you to suffer, to struggle or to be poor. The God Force expects you to eventually become free.

ON PEOPLE'S LACK

HE REASON most people are poorly paid is that they have little skill and they put little true effort into their labor. If you want abundance, start right now by agreeing that you will pump energy into your work, as much as it takes for as long as it takes. Most put the cart before the horse by saying "Give me a pay raise and I'll work harder." First you put the energy in, then you crank up your pay demands. If you go at it the other way you may get little raises, but you won't get major leaps to new levels. If you want to get a pay raise in 30 days, you should dress immaculately, get in half-an-hour early, leave late, work really hard and offer to do extra

THE SECRETS OF LIFE

things for the boss even if he or she
wants you to walk their pet budgie.
After 30 days, go in and ask for a pay
raise because you work hard and
deserve it and if you get a flat "no",
start looking around for another job
because they obviously don't
appreciate your efforts, but
others will.

ON MAKING LIFE SACRED

OW DOES something become sacred? It becomes sacred by people saying, "This is sacred." There is no other way. So Saint Matilda's toenail in a box is just that, until someone says, "This relic is holy and special." So how do you make your life sacred? You say, "This is sacred," and you treat it that way. By making your life special others begin to treat you differently.

ON INNER GUIDANCE

WHAT DO you do if your inner guidance comes up with some bizarre idea like putting your testicles in ice-cold water for a minute as an energy raising technique? At least try it! You never know, it might work. One Australian I know was so energized by that idea he couldn't sleep for 37 hours after doing it. I don't know how long he left them in!

ON FALLING IN LOVE

WHEN WE fall in love, what attracts us most about other people is how different they are to us. Look at all the little "Dudley Moores" who marry Amazonian ladies or the princesses who marry their chauffeurs. Once hitched, we tend to change ourselves to accommodate what we think our partner wants of us, then we try to change them to suit our view of life. So, what starts out as an exciting relationship full of spontaneity and contrast becomes a life of strict regime, making everything seem the same. We wind up "tick-tocking" to each other's tune. It is so simple to criticize our mate for we are close to them, and we know so

THE SECRETS OF LIFE

much about their weaknesses. But in doing so, what we are really saying is that we are not comfortable with ourselves. It is almost impossible to go beyond a weakness by concentrating on it. For by concentrating on it, you energize it. It's better for you both to develop and enhance your strengths. Many women pick weak spouses and in doing so they sentence themselves to a lifetime of struggle. They put into life, "Send me a wet flannel," and sooner or later they pull to themselves a proper "nana." "I'm getting married," they say, and their Mum replies, "That's nice dear, who's the guy?" "Luke." "Luke who?" asks their Mum. "Luke Warm. We'll struggle like crazy and have a lot of luke-warm kids."

ON THE TAO

THERE'S NO book you can study to learn the Tao, because if you read about it in a book, it isn't the Tao. I read the Tao Te Ching and realized I wasn't any the wiser. So to discover the Tao I went out into nature. Every day for three years I woke at 4:30 a.m. and walked in the forest in the dark. By being in the forest in the dark, my mind became centered even though at the beginning I was a bit freaked out. But by doing that discipline of walking I got a perception of energy. I began to understand what the Tao is. The Taoists revere nature because they say it is a pure manifestation of the God Force, uncluttered by emotion or limitation. I finally got it.

THE SECRETS OF LIFE

ON PERCEPTION

PERCEPTION IS demanding of your mind that it notice everything. Walk into a room and force your attention to watch everything, to count everything, to be aware of what is there and what is not there. Force it to focus and take note. Doing so as a mental discipline heightens your overall perceptions of life.

THE SECRETS OF LIFE

ON SELF-EMPOWERMENT

FEAR KEEPS you alive. It's an ally. Treat it with respect. Ram through the fear—ram through the stuff in life. The fear becomes symbolic. Courage is not absence of fear—courage is recognizing fear and operating within it. Fear is the ally that empowers us. Ask yourself, what is the worst thing that can happen?

ON POSITIVE EXPECTANCY

EXPECT THE best. Put your mind, your emotions, and your enthusiasm behind that affirmation. Create yourself in an image that is strong. Where is your mind? See yourself on the other side—having what it is that you want. Your intention gets you to the other side. Focus your attention, be up for it, allow the experience to carry you. Be involved with your inner self. Know how you feel—be emotionally aware. Commit.

ON HIRING OR ASSOCIATING WITH PEOPLE

NCE YOU become more powerful you will want to ensure that the people around you are of the same energy. Create a narrow entrance into your life. Get a new team of people. Execute the old order. Create a new empire. Be shrewd. Keep it clean. Put in a few hurdles so the wimps can't make it into your encampment. That way you and the people around you remain dedicated and strong. It only takes one whiner or bad energy to pollute your whole life.

ON BEING CRAFTY, NOT SNEAKY

CRAFTINESS IS not being sneaky. It's just mastering the craft of humanhood. It's easy to operate in the marketplace of life with shrewdness, and still have honor. Craftiness allows you to maximize your benefits with a minimum of effort. Position yourself on the high ground. Use the information that is available to you. Use it to cut corners. That's the Mongol way.

ON SELF-ACCEPTANCE

STRUGGLERS CRAVE acceptance; they have low self-esteem. This causes them to seek constantly the acceptance and approval of others. Yet, the acknowledgment they seek is rarely forthcoming and is usually dissatisfying even when they get it. This causes frustration. By lacking identity—a sense of knowing and accepting who they are—they shift their attention from what is real (inside of them) to the symbols of life which are not real (outside of them).

THE SECRETS OF LIFE

ON I AM WHAT I AM

YOU HAVE the right to be satisfied with what you have and what you are right now. You have to be happy with your lot right now. There must be lessons to learn here and now. If those lessons are not learned, if you do not accept what you have created for yourself, your energy does not move forward. By resisting, by not adapting to change, you stagnate. Today is part of your life's curriculum. Learn it and tomorrow will look after itself.

ON OPINION

THAT WHICH is struggle to one person is just gentle effort to another. Struggle is always how you feel about something—your opinion, your reaction to the circumstance, not the circumstance itself. To dump struggle you should get used to asking yourself in each circumstance, what is my underlying emotion or opinion here?

ON FLOW

IF THINGS don't flow, ask yourself, "Am I going too fast?" or, "Am I too slow? Is this the right time?" Usually things take longer than we expect them to. This is because we can think faster than we can act. So, ideas have to have time to incubate and come together, especially when you need others to help you materialize your dreams. To make life work you have to face it full-frontal, head out with a good plan and trust in the Great Spirit to deliver. But, head out toward your goal even if it seems a long way off. Nothing will carry you. You will usually have to carry yourself.

THE SECRETS OF LIFE

ON YOUR LIFE AND THE CAST OF CHARACTERS

T O GO beyond struggle you first have to be able to accept the help of others and secondly you have to choose your characters carefully. If you find yourself in a campaign with the cast already set, you must become a crafty "general" and get the most out of your people given the circumstances, the goals, and what the budget allows. Never be afraid to let someone go if they are not right.

ON CHANGE IS NATURAL

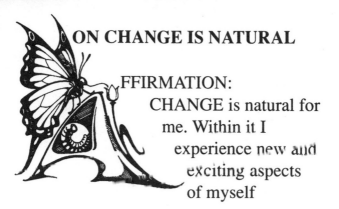

AFFIRMATION:
CHANGE is natural for
me. Within it I
experience new and
exciting aspects
of myself

ON KARMIC LAW

A person who violates the rights of others and infringes on their freedom creates an energy of restriction around himself. That, in turn, pulls to him others who will violate his rights. It is not crime and punishment in the sense of retribution for sin, it is more energy in motion, its consequences, if you like.

THE SECRETS OF LIFE

ON NUTRITIONAL DISCIPLINE

There is no faster way of raising your energy than adopting good eating habits. The body's nutritional needs become clear and you gradually become your own healer. The healing process cannot occur unless you maintain an alkaline balance in the food you eat.

ON DISCIPLINE

DISCIPLINE IS good for you—it helps you control your life. But too much of the same discipline eventually spins you into the laws of diminishing returns. If you follow the same discipline for years and years, eventually it has no more power for you, and it will become an energy drag rather than an energy booster. Personal discipline is like a muscle. You need to squeeze it and let go, then squeeze it some more to keep your disciplines fresh. Change them often, and also have periods of no discipline at all. That will give you the best results.

THE SECRETS OF LIFE

ON WAR

WAR IS a drag, but it is a part of human nature to be war-like. We should recognize that and treat it as a disease like drug addiction. If I were Secretary General of the United Nations, I'd set aside a bit of land like the Gobi desert and I'd make everyone go and have their punch-ups on that spot. I'd sell tickets and hot dogs and make it into an event. And I would limit the war to three days. An international committee would declare the winner. We could have medal ceremonies and national anthems, and Nike or Adidas could endorse the boots and so on. It's not fair when they have wars downtown; it messes with the traffic.

THE SECRETS OF LIFE

ON WORLD PEACE

S O MUCH of life is just a matter of how you look at things— what your opinion is. Think about world peace. Right now, everybody's trottin' about waxing lyrical about how we've gotta have world peace. And, a lot of people are all upset and in anguish about the whole thing. If there's five billion people in the world and there's approximately five million people at war, that leaves 4,995 million people who aren't at war today. Perhaps we've got world peace without even knowin' it.

ON FLOWERS

THERE ARE no words to describe the exceptional beauty of a flower glistening with the morning dew. Have you ever stared into a flower for ten minutes or so? After a while you begin to see universes in its center. It seems to me that each flower gives off a tone. It isn't audible in the normal sense but if you are very still you can hear it in your mind. It seems to me that the spirits that exist in the flowers must be very pure. I must say, if I were very small that's where I'd go for a rest and a little nap.

THE SECRETS OF LIFE

ON GAIETY

HERE IS a gaiety to life. There's a carefree beauty, and as you begin to develop a philosophy of life that is carefree, you become this wonderful scamp who is organized and a little disorganized, who's on time and a little late, who is reliable and a little unreliable.

ON THE LUSHNESS OF LIFE

THEY SAY that the lush things of life make you fat. And they are probably right. But if you constantly deny yourself the lush sensual things of life, eventually your spirit gets too thin. It is better that you are a little overweight and that your heart is full and rich with life's experiences, than that you wind up with a thin body and an anorexic spirit.

THE SECRETS OF LIFE

ON ANIMALS

PERSONALLY, I'VE never met an animal I didn't like. I can't say the same for all the folk I've met. When I look into a dog's eyes I see the spark of God in there, and that spark is saying to me, "Stupot, try to be as honorable and natural and pure as this dog for I, the God Force, am inside this animal and it is in me. And when I set the evolution of this world into being, I, the God Force, had to think of an unobtrusive way of watching what is going on. I chose the animal kingdom for it is humble and honorable, and it is through the eyes of the animals that I watch and evaluate the progress or lack of progress that humans attain."

THE SECRETS OF LIFE

ON HORSES AND RACING

THERE IS nothing softer in the whole world than a horse's nose. And there is nothing more pleasing than a hundred bucks on the first soft nose past the post. I love racing. It has to be one of the most glorious ways of paying the rent ever devised.

ON CASINOS

WHEN I was younger I used to go into casinos, try my luck, lose and go home again. I put it down to the fact that casinos have to win in order to stay in business. Then one day it struck me that casinos also have to lose money in order to stay in business, for if they never lost they'd have no customers. That thought inspired me. I was like Saint Paul on the road to Damascus: I suddenly saw the light. I decided to really learn cards and it wasn't long before I went from mug punter to pro' player. Since then I have been to almost all of the famous casinos of the world. They very graciously agreed to pay for my visit and to slip me a little "folding

THE SECRETS OF LIFE

money" that they insisted I use to enrich my travels. Sweet of them really. God, how I love casinos.

ON DANCING

KNOW that dancing is nothing more than organized wobbling, but not having a lot of natural rhythm in my bones, the pleasure I experience in dancing is more than wiped out by the silliness I feel as I try to get things to wiggle coherently. But I'm willin' to keep trying. Sometimes, I wish I were African.

THE SECRETS OF LIFE

ON BEING
WHAT YOU ARE

 AM what I am.
I am what I need!
Robyne Wilde

THE SECRETS OF LIFE

About Stuart Wilde

Author, lecturer, Stuart Wilde is one of the real characters of the Self-Help, Human Potential Movement. His style is humorous, controversial, poignant, and transformational. He has written eight books, including the very successful Taos Quintet, which are considered classics in their genre. They are: *Miracles*, *Affirmations*, *The Force*, *The Quickening*, and *The Trick to Money is Having Some*. His books have been translated into nine languages.

Stuart Wilde travels, lecturing in ninety cities around the world. He is the originator of the Warrior's Wisdom seminar intensive, considered by many as one of the most impacting self-help courses of its kind in the world.

He lives with his wife and young child at the airport.

We hope you enjoyed this Hay House book. If you would like to receive a free catalog featuring additional Hay House books and products, or if you would like information about the Hay Foundation, please write to:

Hay House, Inc.
1154 E. Dominguez St.
P.O. Box 6204
Carson, CA 90749-6204
(800) 654-5126

◆ ◆ ◆ ◆ ◆ ◆ ◆ ◆ ◆ ◆

STUART WILDE International Tour and Seminar Information:

For information on Stuart Wilde's latest tour and seminar dates in the USA and Canada, contact:

White Dove International
P.O. Box 1000, Taos, NM 87571
(505) 758-0500 — phone
(505) 758-2265 — fax